THE ADVENTURES OF RHONA THE UNICORN IN SCOTLAND

Colouring Book

Veropa Press
2019

Copyright © 2019 by Veropa Press

All rights reserved. No part of this publication may be reproduced, stored in a retrieval system or transmitted, in any form or by any means, electronic, mechanical, photocopying, recording or otherwise, without permission in writing from the publisher.

The Adventures of Rhona The Unicorn in Scotland. Colouring Book
ISBN 978-1-5272-4068-1

For wholesale inquiries, please contact us: veropapress@gmail.com
We would love to discuss the opportunity!

Imagine an enchanted forest far away.
Far away from the modern world and its roads and cars and buildings and people.
In the deepest part of that enchanted forest is where the unicorns live.

Surrounded by nature, unicorn families live happy, peaceful lives. But there was one young unicorn who longed to discover what lay beyond the enchanted forest...

Rhona the unicorn begged her mum and dad to let her go exploring.
When they eventually agreed, Rhona jumped in the air with excitement.
And so she started planning her first adventure by making a map of all the places to visit...
on her tour of Scotland!

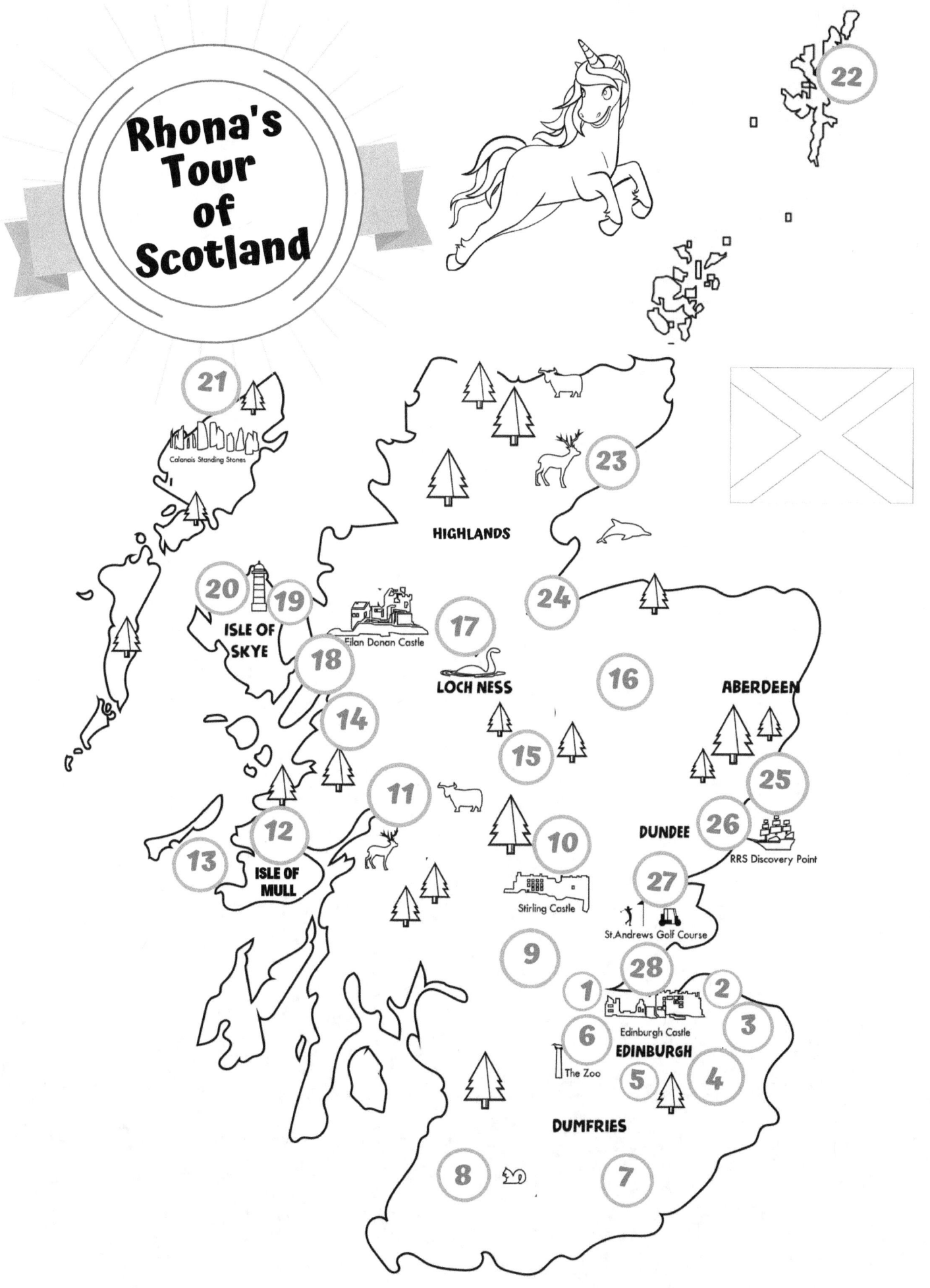

Here is the list of Rhona's travel destinations.
Find them on the map

1. Royal Mile, Edinburgh
2. Edinburgh Castle and Princes Street Gardens
3. Greyfriars Bobby, Edinburgh
4. Calton Hill, Edinburgh
5. Christmas Market, Edinburgh
6. Edinburgh Zoo

7. Sheep, Dumfries and Galloway
8. Red Squirrel, Galloway Forest Park, Dumfries and Galloway
9. The Kelpies, Falkirk
10. Stirling Castle
11. Red Deer, Glencoe
12. Otter, Isle of Mull

13. Colony of Puffins, Isle of Lunga
14. Glenfinnan Viaduct, Jacobite Steam Train
15. Highland Cow, Cairngorms National Park
16. Mountain Hare, Cromdale Hills
17. Loch Ness, Urquhart Castle and Nessie
18. Eilean Donan Castle, Western Highlands

19. Neist Point Lighthouse, Isle of Skye
20. Grey Seals and Dunvegan Castle, Isle of Skye
21. Calanais Standing Stones, Isle of Lewis
22. Grey Seals, Shetland and Orkney Islands
23. Dunrobin Castle and Falconry, Golspie
24. Dolphins, Chanonry Point

25. Dunnottar Castle, Stonehaven
26. Discovery, The Royal Research Ship, Discovery Point in Dundee
27. The Old Course, St Andrews
28. The Forth Bridge

1

Royal Mile, Edinburgh

2

Edinburgh Castle and Princes Street Gardens

3

Greyfriars Bobby, Edinburgh

4

Calton Hill, Edinburgh

5

Christmas Market, Edinburgh

6

Edinburgh Zoo

7

Sheep,
Dumfries and Galloway

8

Red Squirrels, Galloway Forest Park, Dumfries and Galloway

9

The Kelpies, Falkirk

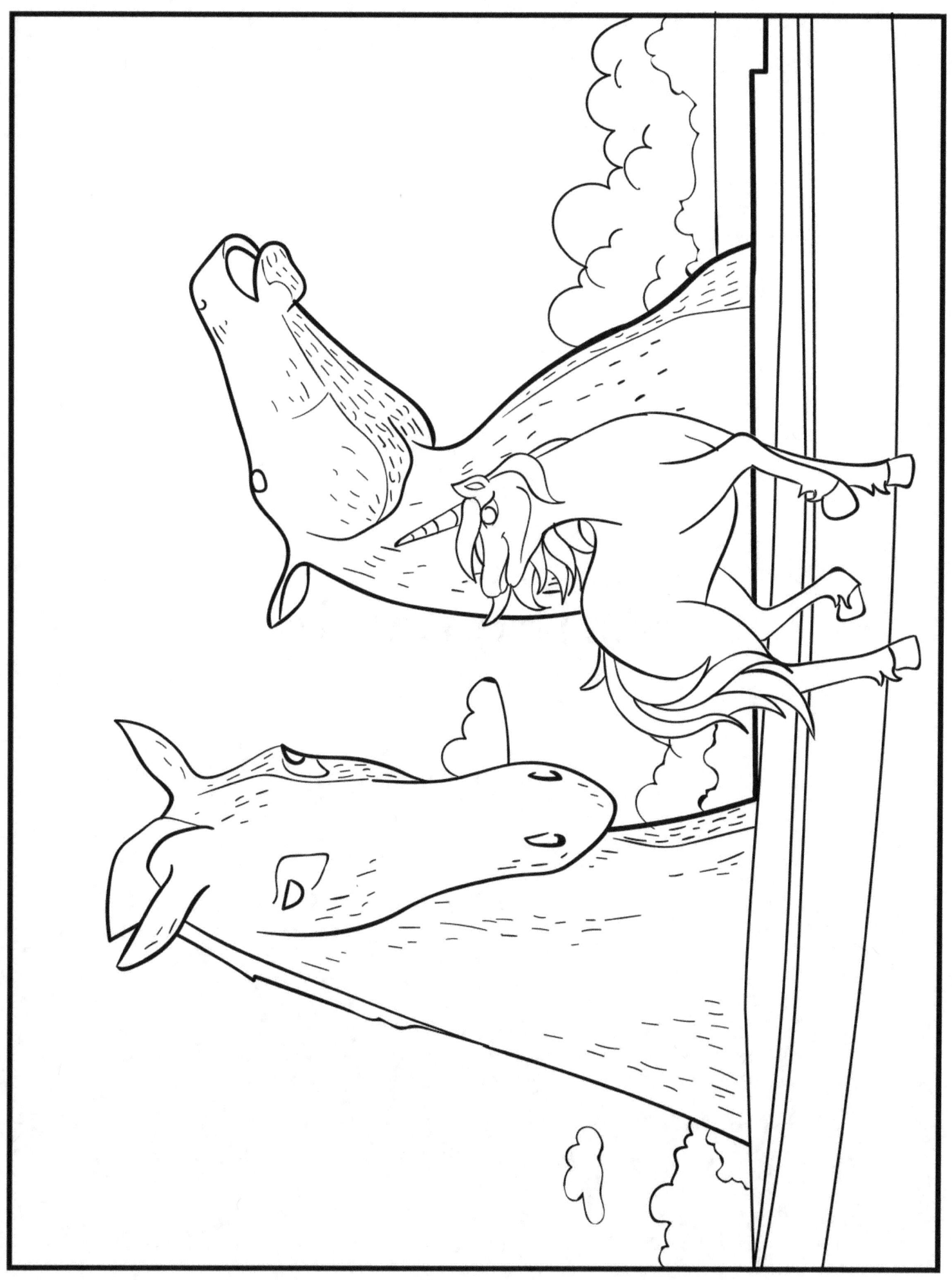

10

Stirling Castle

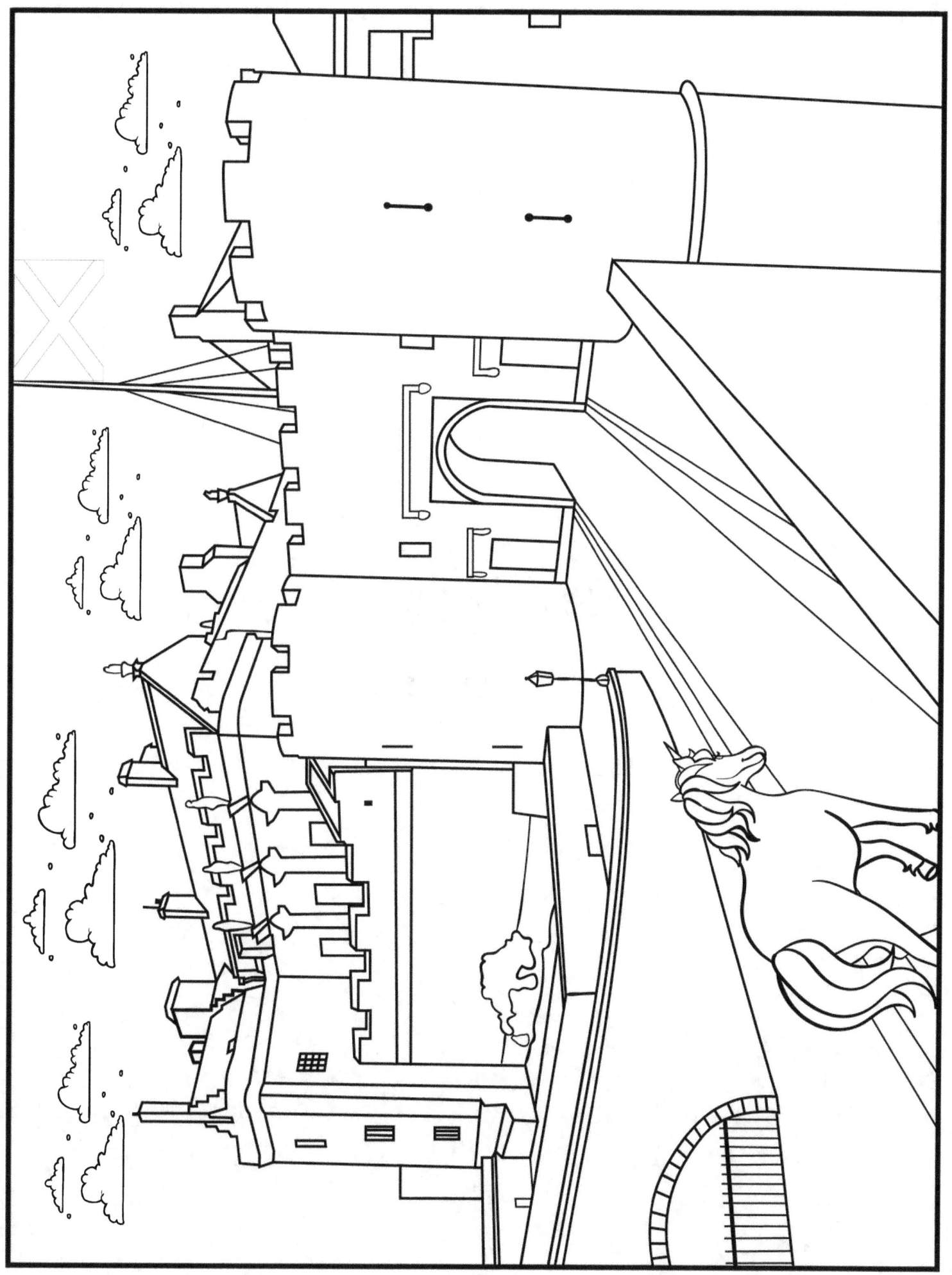

11

Red Deer, Glencoe

12
Otter, Isle of Mull

13

Colony of Puffins, Isle of Lunga

14

Glenfinnan Viaduct, Jacobite Steam Train

15

Highland Cow, Cairngorms National Park

16

Mountain Hare, Cromdale Hills

17

Loch Ness, Urquhart Castle and Nessie

18

Eilean Donan Castle, The Western Highlands

19

Neist Point Lighthouse, Isle of Skye

20

Grey Seals and Dunvegan Castle, Isle of Skye

21

Calanais Standing Stones, Isle of Lewis

22

Grey Seals, Shetland and Orkney

23

Dunrobin Castle and Falconry, Golspie

24

Dolphins, Chanonry Point

25

Dunnottar Castle, Stonehaven

26
Discovery, The Royal Research Ship, Discovery Point in Dundee

27
The Old Course, St Andrews

28

The Forth Bridge

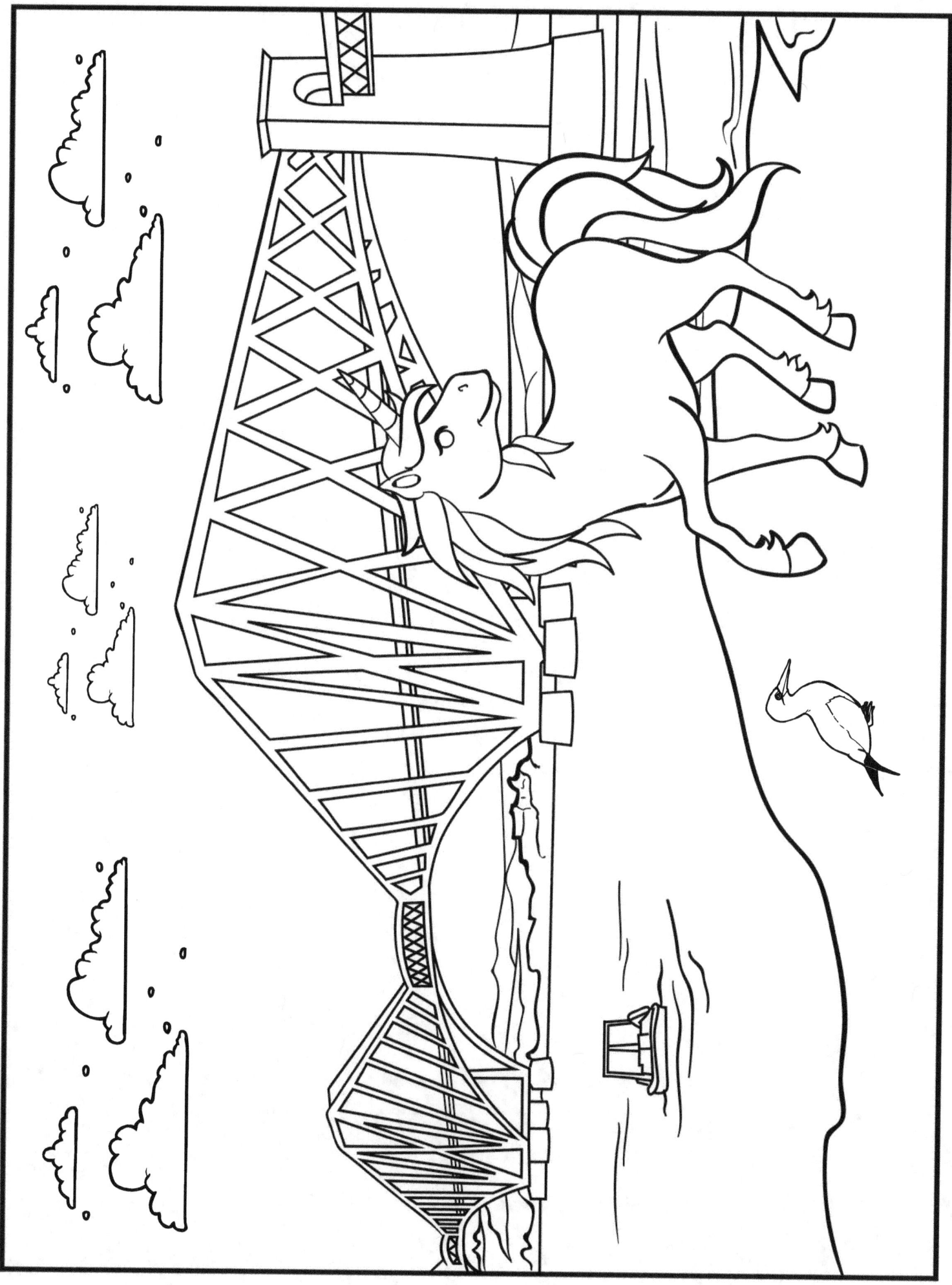